SPACE LIBRARY
SPACE SATELLITES
GREGORY VOGT

FRANKLIN WATTS
NEW YORK LONDON TORONTO SYDNEY

Each new generation of humankind has had the challenge of a frontier. The frontier for to-day's children is outer space; it beckons with unlimited experiences. It is the frontier of my children, and I dedicate this book to them.

Kirsten, Allison and Catherine Vogt

First published in the USA
by Franklin Watts Inc.
387 Park Ave. South
New York, N.Y. 10016

First published in 1987 by
Franklin Watts
12a Golden Square
London W1R 4BA

First published in Australia
by Franklin Watts
Australia
14 Mars Road
Lane Cove, NSW 2066

US ISBN: 0-531-10141-X
UK ISBN: 0-86313 479 3
Library of Congress
Catalog Card No: 86-13310

Designed by Michael Cooper

Photo credits:
All photos from NASA, except for the following: page 4 (left) The Granger Collection; page 5, Bettmann Archive; page 6 (upper right) Novosti/Science Photo Library; page 8 (middle) NASDA; page 8 (bottom) Scientific Imagery, Department of Communications; pages 10 and 11 (bottom) ESA; page 11 (top) NASDA

CONTENTS

The First Satellites   4
The Early Launches   6
Nuts and Bolts   8
The Clouds Below   10
Reaching the World   12
Painting by Numbers   14
Red Trees, Blue Cities   16
Telescopes on Satellites   18
Seeing the Invisible   20
Mayday! Mayday!   22
The High Ground   24
Fixing Costly Mistakes   26
The Next Generation   28
Important Dates   30
Satellite Scoreboard   30
Glossary   31
Index   32

THE FIRST SATELLITES

On a summer evening in 1666, an apple fell from a tree near Woolsthorpe, England. It started someone thinking. On October 4, 1957, a 57-cm (23-in) diameter, 84-kg (184-lb) metal ball was rocketed into orbit about the Earth. Nearly 300 years separate these two closely related monumental events. How were they related? To find out, we must examine each one.

When the apple fell, Sir Isaac Newton, a famous scientist, was sitting under the tree. Legend has it that the apple hit him on the head. Actually, it missed and made a soft thud on the ground, but that was enough to attract Newton's attention. For years, Newton and many other scientists before him had wondered what kept the Moon and the planets in orbit. The apple fall triggered the important realization that a force, gravity, attracts all bodies in the universe to each other, pulling apples to the ground and holding the Moon and the planets in their orbits.

In 1729, two years after his death, a book containing Newton's theories was published. In it Newton demonstrated how an artificial satellite could be launched above the Earth. He pictured the Earth with a high mountain. A cannon on top of the mountain fired shots parallel to the ground. Each time the cannon was fired, more gunpowder was used and the shot went farther before striking the ground.

The original of this drawing, which appeared in 1728, showed paths that a projectile could take. Each path depends on the velocity with which the projectile is launched; when the velocity is great enough, it will go into orbit around the Earth, just as an artificial satellite does.

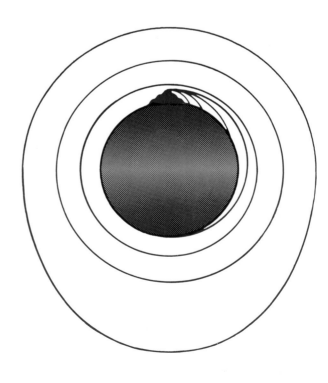

An apple's fall inspired Sir Isaac Newton's research into the force of gravity.

Because the Earth is round, the shots curved around it. According to Newton's theory a shot could eventually go fast enough to circle the Earth completely and come back to the mountaintop. Newton showed that the force pushing the cannon shot outward was balanced by the inward pull of gravity. Consequently, the shot could circle the Earth. It was exactly this principle that the Soviet Union took advantage of in 1957 to launch Sputnik 1.

To put Sputnik into orbit, the Soviets used a powerful rocket to raise it high above the Earth and shoot it parallel to the ground at a very high speed. At 161 km (100 mi) up, a satellite must travel at 28,240 km/h (17,600 mph) just to keep the forces balanced.

Sputnik 1 was placed in an egg-shaped orbit that went as high as 947 km (590 mi) and as low as 228 km (141 mi). Little was then known about the nearby region of outer space, and Sputnik's orbit helped scientists learn about the density of the atmosphere at different altitudes. Two radio transmitters on board sent back information, including the temperature of the satellite itself.

Three months after its launch, Sputnik 1's orbit decayed and the satellite was destroyed during its fiery reentry into the Earth's atmosphere. Although Sputnik was a relatively simple device and did little more than prove Newton's idea, it set off an incredible chain of events. The space race had begun.

Sputnik 1, the world's first artificial satellite, rests in a stand just before being loaded onto a rocket for its launch into space.

THE EARLY LAUNCHES

In the United States, there was great disappointment that the Russians had won the race to launch the first satellite. Even greater was the fear that if the Russians could launch satellites they could also put atomic bombs into orbit that could drop down on the United States at any moment. It was out of this fear that the United States redoubled its efforts to launch its own satellite.

The first U.S. attempt to launch a satellite ended in a spectacular failure. The launch took place on December 6, 1957, at Cape Canaveral in Florida just two months after Sputnik 1. A 22.7-m- (72 ft) tall needlelike Vanguard rocket stood on the launch pad ready to climb into space. However, two seconds after ignition, having barely moved at all, the rocket lost thrust and blew itself to pieces in a huge fireball. This failure was especially embarrassing since Sputnik 2 had been launched on November 3, and the Russians now had two satellites in orbit.

(Far left) The first attempted American satellite launch ended when the Vanguard launch vehicle exploded. (Below) Laika, the first animal to orbit Earth, is prepared for launch. A harness is attached with instruments that measured the dog's pulse, blood pressure and breathing rate. (Bottom) The pencil-shaped Explorer 1 was the first successful U.S. satellite.

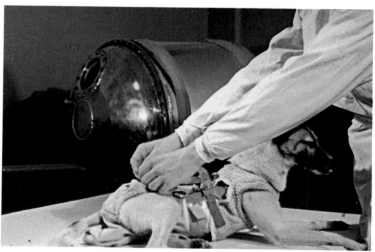

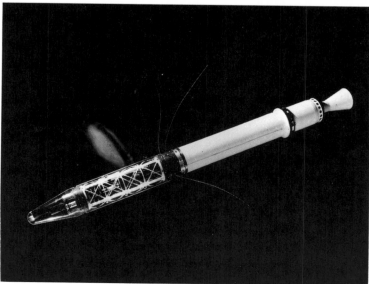

Sputnik 2 was the first satellite to carry a passenger. It was a small dog named Laika. Laika's space home was a satellite that weighed a whopping 509 kg (1,120 lb)! Laika paved the way for future human astronauts by showing that it was possible to remain alive in space. Unfortunately, the satellite carried life support supplies for only a few days and unable to survive any longer, Laika died in orbit.

Following a second Vanguard failure two months after the first, the first American satellite was finally launched on January 31, 1958. A modified Redstone missile, later named Jupiter C, carried a 13.6-kg (30-lb) pencil-shaped satellite into orbit. This was Explorer 1 and, like the Russian satellite, it carried instruments and radio transmitters. Sputnik 1 had been a ball with four antennas sticking out. It rolled as it orbited. Explorer 1's pencil shape meant that it had to spin like a bullet to remain stable in space. It too had four antennas. Explorer 1's orbit was egg-shaped, like that of Sputnik 1, and climbed as high as 2,512 km (1,573 mi) and descended to as low as 360 km (224 mi).

The instruments on Explorer 1 measured cosmic radiation, temperature in space and micrometeoroid hits. These instruments enabled two very important discoveries about outer space to be made. One was the presence of highly charged radioactive particles trapped in huge belts by the Earth's magnetic field. Sputnik 2 had sensed radiation, but Explorer 1 definitely confirmed its presence. The discovery was named the Van Allen Radiation Belt, after the scientist who designed the satellite's instrument.

The second discovery was that the danger of micrometeoroids in the near space environment of Earth was not as great as once feared. Some scientists had thought that high-speed micrometeoroids would pierce holes through satellites and possibly kill astronauts of the future but Explorer 1 recorded only seven minor hits in its first month.

NUTS AND BOLTS

Now, after thirty years of satellite launchings, nearly 3,500 satellites have been launched for eighteen countries and five international organizations. Almost half of those satellites remain in orbit today. Satellites have taken on nearly every shape and size imaginable. Some are as small as a grapefruit, and others are as large as a house. Satellites have been launched to conduct scientific studies in outer space, to study the Earth's weather, to prospect for minerals, to examine the world's oceans, to relay telephone calls and television, to spy on other countries or to study pollution.

In spite of differences in size and appearance, most satellites share a few basic parts. To begin with, some form of shell or framework is needed to hold the satellite together and protect its systems from conditions in outer space. Satellite instruments must either be designed to work in a condition of zero pressure or be sealed off in a shell. The shell protects the instruments from damage by micrometeoroids careening at speeds of thousands of kilometers per hour as well as great temperature changes.

The purpose of a satellite is to do work. Scientific satellites have instruments on board to take pictures of the Earth or probe outward into space to measure magnetic fields and detect radiation. To make the instruments work properly, a computer system directs all satellite functions and interprets new instructions from the controllers on the ground. Satellites designed for communications have radio repeating equipment to relay telephone calls and television programs to other parts of the world.

Japanese technicians prepare for the 1977 launch of the Engineering Test Satellite–II to search for information needed for future satellites.

The large solar cell panels powering the Canadian Communications Technology Satellite stretch 17 m (56 ft) from tip to tip. With their wide variety of parts, satellites have weird shapes, with instrument booms, antennas, and solar panels poking out in all directions.

West German technicians give the Helios-B one final check before shipping it to the NASA Kennedy Space Center for launch. Helios satellites explore the complex processes taking place in space near the Sun.

Most satellites must be aimed in a particular direction to operate properly, and for this an attitude control system is present. In one system, electric motors spin the satellite rapidly before it is released from its launching rocket. Another system uses small bursts from rocket engines placed around the satellite. This keeps the satellite from drifting off course.

Providing electrical energy for the satellite is the job of the power supply. Power is provided by batteries, solar cells that convert sunlight to electricity, or small nuclear power plants.

The last major satellite part is the communications system. Antennas are used to send and receive data and instructions.

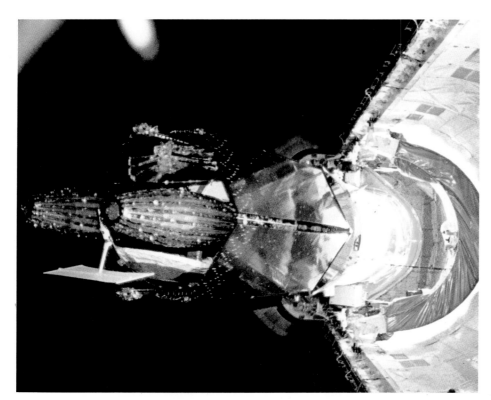

NASA's Tracking and Data Relay Satellite (TDRS) was deployed from the Space Shuttle *Challenger* on April 4, 1984. A second planned TDRS was destroyed during the tragic explosion of *Challenger* on January 28, 1986.

THE CLOUDS BELOW

Before satellites, meteorologists (weather scientists) had to depend solely upon a complex system of weather stations around the world to determine what was happening and to predict changes. The atmosphere is like a gigantic jigsaw puzzle, and the measurements they took of it were the pieces. Unfortunately, the picture changed faster than it was possible to put the pieces together.

Satellites changed all this because satellite camera systems could look down and take pictures of large segments of the clouds. Huge swirls and long streaks of clouds could be seen that were excellent indicators of the weather. Dense cloud masses indicated rain or snow. Swirls might be hurricanes or typhoons. By looking at pictures taken hours apart, forecasters could see the clouds' movements, indicating wind speed and direction. Weather satellites also carried instruments that measured air temperature and the temperature of the surface water in the oceans.

Weather satellites come in many forms and have been launched by the United States, the Soviet Union and the European Space Agency (ESA). Satellites have been placed in low orbits to get close-up views of the Earth or in high orbits to see large areas.

Low weather satellites are placed in polar orbits. As they circle, they see a strip of atmosphere beneath them a few hundred kilometers wide running from pole to pole. By itself, one strip doesn't mean much, but each new orbit adds another. At the end of the day, all the strips are joined together revealing the clouds over the entire Earth. High weather satellites can see nearly one-third of the Earth. With just three high satellites equally spaced above the equator, the entire Earth can be seen at one time.

(Left) This weather image was made by ESA's Meteosat stationed over the Atlantic Ocean. All of Africa and parts of Europe and South America are visible. Clouds appear bright white. (Below) Meteosat recorded water vapor in the Earth's atmosphere. Darker areas show low level atmospheric water. No land is visible.

Japan launched the Geostationary Meteorological Satellite-2 in 1981 to provide Japan and fifteen other Asian and western Pacific nations with weather forecast data.

Whether in a polar orbit or high above the equator, weather satellites look at sunlight reflected off the clouds and take pictures of them. The pictures are then broken down into tiny bits of information which are transmitted by radio to ground stations, where they are reassembled into pictures for the forecasters. Pictures can even be taken at night by looking at infrared radiation produced by heat stored in the clouds. Pictures from high satellites are assembled one after another, making time-lapse sequences of cloud movements.

(Left) An infrared radiation image of Earth reveals temperatures. Cold, high clouds appear light and warmer clouds are darker. Africa is highlighted with false red and yellow. (Below) A close-up view of the cloud patterns over the Mediterranean Sea. Land masses are colored brown and green by a computer.

REACHING THE WORLD

Communications satellites are placed in geosynchronous orbits 35,800 km (22,300 mi) above the Earth. This is a special orbit directly above the Earth's equator. A satellite in that orbit is aimed eastward so that its motion exactly matches the Earth's rotation. In other words, the satellite stays over the same point on the Earth at all times. You might visualize this by standing up with one of your arms outstretched and your hand in a fist. Your fist is the satellite and you are the Earth. Turn around in a circle. The satellite orbits you as you turn, but it is always straight out from your shoulder. The advantage of geosynchronous orbits is that satellite antennas on the ground don't have to be moved continually to follow the satellite. Aim them once and they are set. Another advantage is that the satellite is high enough to relay communications over large portions of the Earth at one time.

While there are many different communications satellites in orbit, they generally are of two kinds. The first is a passive satellite that merely reflects radio signals. Echo I and II were passive U.S. satellites of the early 1960s. Both were very large space balloons made of an aluminum-coated plastic as large as 41 m (135 ft) in diameter. Radio transmitters on the ground beamed up signals that bounced back to receivers elsewhere. Although this kind of satellite is very reliable, because it has no electronic parts which could fail, it requires powerful transmitters and sensitive receivers on the ground.

The second and most common kind of communications satellite is active, because it has equipment onboard to amplify the power of incoming signals before they are relayed back. A good example of this is the EUTELSAT system of satellites built and launched by the European Space Agency. The system consists of three satellites (and two spares) designed to last seven years. They are placed in orbits that enable them to be seen by all of Europe.

(Left) The 9-m (30-ft) diameter antenna of ATS-6 gives the satellite an umbrellalike appearance. The large antenna made it possible to reduce the size of the antennas at the ground receiving station. (Below) The Echo I satellite dwarfs the group of people standing near its base. Made of aluminum-coated plastic, the radio-signal-reflecting satellite unfolded from a tight package and was inflated in orbit.

Many remote villages in India got their first look at television from signals relayed by the ATS-6 satellite.

The purpose of the EUTELSAT is to relay television programs and long-distance telephone calls. The satellites relay 10,000 telephone calls and two television channels simultaneously, with up to twenty extra channels of commentary for each of the different languages used in Europe.

The EUTELSAT system is really a part of a much larger system of communications satellites forming a complete ring over the Earth's equator. We use these satellites directly or indirectly every day. Many long-distance telephone calls travel through space via satellite without the parties on either side of the conversation being aware that it is happening. World news and thousands of television programs are relayed daily to television stations. Scientific data, hotel and airline reservations, computer talk and financial data for banks also take the high route through space.

A Canadian communications satellite is popped spinning out of the Space Shuttle's payload bay before being boosted by an attached rocket motor into geosynchronous orbit.

PAINTING BY NUMBERS

Taking pictures of the Earth from space has always been a popular and useful pastime of astronauts in satellites orbiting the Earth. Some unmanned satellites have been constructed especially for the purpose of looking at the Earth's surface. They have given us a new view of a familiar place.

In 1972 a new satellite, called Landsat, was launched by the United States to study the land. Landsat 1 was the first of four very successful satellites that have taken pictures of virtually every bit of land surface on the earth. The pictures are beautiful but surprising because these satellites did not use normal cameras. Instead, they used scanning devices and television systems, which produced pictures with strange colors. Trees show up as red, water becomes black and cities become blue. Though strange to look at, the colors have special meaning to geologists, agricultural researchers, environmental scientists and city planners.

From hundreds of kilometers above Earth, Landsat 4 transmitted this image of the Washington, D.C., area. Washington is the light-bluish area just left of the middle. The Potomac River stretches to the south of the city, joining with Chesapeake Bay to the east.

Landsat produces pictures by orbiting the earth in a pathway that lets it move in a near-polar orbit. As a Landsat travels southward, it passes on the sunlit side of the earth. It returns northward on the dark side and then begins a new orbit southward in daylight again. Each time it heads south, its camera systems begin taking pictures. One of the systems it uses is called the multispectral scanner. It is usually shortened to "MSS." The MSS takes pictures in a manner similar to the way you read a book. You start in the upper left of the page and scan your eyes to the right. Then you drop down a line and do it again. Eventually, you get to the end of the page and you have seen it all by scanning.

Landsat's MSS has a mirror that moves from side to side as the satellite moves southward. Light from the Earth passes through a prism on the satellite that breaks it up into the colors of the rainbow. Light detectors are aimed at some of those colors and measure the brightness of the light. Each color is converted into a number.

On Earth, computers take the numbers sent down by the satellite and arrange them in their correct order in a picture. Because several different colors were measured for each point on the picture, the computer has to average them all together before printing the picture. In the end, scientists are able to study the Earth from space in brilliant but false colors. Each color can tell scientists many things about the places they are looking at that they couldn't see with their own eyes.

(Far left) Landsat 3 with its solar panels spread open before its launch in 1978. Scanning systems for making images of Earth are on the base of the satellite. (Above) Landsat 4 featured improvements in the sensor systems over the first three Landsats. This enabled it to make more detailed images than before and to gather new data.

RED TREES, BLUE CITIES

What can be seen from space? To answer this question, we must first go back to the picture-taking process for a moment. Scan lines from the MSS and from television systems are broken down into individual points. Each point, called a pixel (for "picture element"), represents a spot on the Earth. The most advanced Landsat produces pixels that are 30 m (33 yards) across. With a spot this size, most details of interest to scientists are visible. Large buildings and roads, rivers and even rock formations can be picked out from the pictures.

Geologists look at satellite pictures to see the shape of the land. They can see mountains and valleys and how the different types of rock lie against each other. Subtle straight lines may indicate the place of an ancient earthquake. The colors of the rocks and of the soil that lies on top can tell what minerals might be present.

Hydrologists, scientists who study the Earth's water supplies, are eager to look at pictures that show the amount of snow coverage in winter. For many parts of the world, winter mountain snow turns into summer drinking water and irrigation water for the valleys below. Knowing the coverage helps them determine whether or not water rationing will be necessary during the next summer.

A more detailed close-up of the pixels in the Washington picture on the preceding page shows the downtown area. The clover-shaped lake in the center is the Tidal Basin, and the white streak to the right is the Capitol Mall, lined with museums and government buildings.

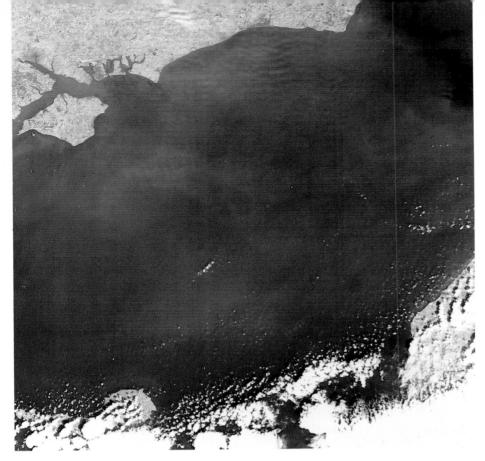

A Landsat picture showing southern England and parts of France is partially obscured by clouds. Normandy is on the lower left. The Isle of Wight stands out in the upper left corner of the frame. Brighton is along the coast just about in the middle of the picture.

Many forms of pollution are visible from space. Oil, illegally dumped at sea by tankers, leaves a very apparent streak in the water that can be used to trace the guilty parties. Air pollution shows up as a cloudlike haze that may stretch out in a line for kilometers. By looking at pollution from the vantage point of space, environmental scientists can assess damages and measure long-range effects.

Researchers are trying to predict crop production for entire countries from satellite pictures in the hope of enabling the world to foresee local food shortages that could lead to large-scale famine. Seafood supplies can be studied by looking for phytoplankton, which are microscopic floating plants coloring large areas of the oceans.

Piecing together hundreds of Landsat images has yielded a false-color photomosaic look at the United States. The red in the picture represents vegetation.

TELESCOPES ON SATELLITES

The air surrounding Earth is not as transparent as it seems. Heat currents and dust particles in the atmosphere cause shimmering or twinkling of the light from stars. Faint, wispy clouds may partially block light. The details astronomers want remain hidden.

One solution to the problem is to climb above the atmosphere and place a telescope on a satellite orbiting the Earth. The telescope is then above the filtering effects of the atmosphere. It can also be used at any time, not just on clear nights. Such a telescope is the Edwin P. Hubble Space Telescope, which NASA plans to launch in the payload bay of the Space Shuttle. (Hubble was an astronomer who made important discoveries about galaxies.) Once in orbit 600 km (373 mi) above Earth, the Shuttle will release the telescope and large solar panels will unfold, providing electricity to operate the telescope's instruments.

The main part of the telescope is its 2.4-m- (94.5 in) diameter magnifying mirror. Although this mirror is less than half the diameter of some of the largest telescopes on Earth, it will be many times more effective because it will operate above the Earth's atmosphere.

Orbiting high above the filtering effects of Earth's atmosphere, the Space Telescope peers into the depths of the universe.

This artist's impression shows the Space Telescope tilted up in the Shuttle's payload bay just before its release. The solar panels for providing electric power are still folded.

The Space Shuttle will make periodic visits to the Space Telescope for routine maintenance and replacement of obsolete instruments. The Space Telescope will be able to peer into space seven times further and look into a volume of space 350 times larger than the biggest telescopes on Earth.

The light gathered by the large mirror at the far end of the 13.1-m- (43.5 ft) long telescope barrel will be reflected forward to a smaller mirror, which will aim it right back toward a small hole in the large mirror. Just beyond that hole is the place where the gathered light will focus. There, an optical assembly with five instruments will divide the light into tiny points. Each point will then be converted to electronic signals that will be transmitted to Earth by radio at a rate of up to one megabit (one million bits) per second. Computers waiting on the ground will convert the signals back into pictures and other scientific data.

Astronomers expect the Space Telescope to enable them to answer many important questions. Orbiting high above the filtering veil of our atmosphere, the Space Telescope will greatly sharpen our view and provide the needed data.

SEEING THE INVISIBLE

Different astronomical satellites do different jobs. To look at X-rays from space, there are the Uhuru and Ariel satellites, Netherlands Astronomy Satellite and the three High Energy Astronomy Observatories. Ultraviolet light is observed with the Ultraviolet Explorer. Infrared light is observed with the Infrared Astronomical Satellite (IRAS). Each of these satellites concentrates on just one part of the total spectrum of radiations that exist. However, when measurements from each are compared, a picture of our universe is produced that is very different from optical telescopes.

IRAS was a joint scientific project sponsored by the Netherlands, the United Kingdom, and the United States. It was launched in a polar orbit on January 25, 1983, and ended its service ten months later.

IRAS was designed to scan the whole sky and look for infrared radiation. Infrared is the kind of invisible light that is associated with heat. To make it sensitive to very-low-temperature infrared radiations, IRAS carried a large tank of very cold liquid helium to cool the infrared detectors close to absolute zero.

Intended for studying the ultraviolet light given off by objects in space, the International Ultraviolet Explorer (IUE) satellite is a joint project of the United States, the United Kingdom and the ESA.

An artist's drawing of the International Ultraviolet Explorer in Earth orbit

During its lifespan, IRAS observed about 20,000 galaxies, 130,000 stars and 90,000 other objects and star clusters. It discovered regions where stars were being born and discovered what could possibly be other solar systems of planets orbiting distant stars. One of these stars is Vega. IRAS located a shell or ring of large particles surrounding the star, some as large as asteroids. Because Vega is a relatively young star, these particles have not had a chance to come together in large planets like those we have around our sun.

Later, IRAS found more than 40 additional stars that appeared to have the same characteristics as Vega. If additional research confirms these discoveries, it will mean that solar systems are relatively common in space. IRAS and the other astronomical satellites provide pieces of important information that astronomers use to piece together a picture of our universe.

IRAS detected more than 250,000 sources of infrared light in the Milky Way galaxy. The center of the galaxy is the bright-red plane running across the picture.

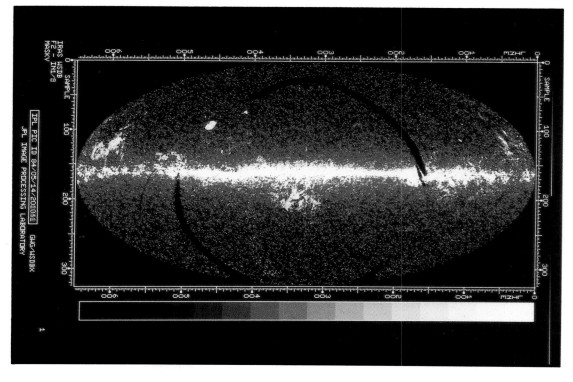

MAYDAY! MAYDAY!

What might start out as a pleasant sea voyage could end in disaster if the weather changes drastically. Events can change so quickly that it may not be possible to use the radio to send out the international distress signal "Mayday!"

In 1984, six fishermen got into trouble on the Mediterranean Sea when foul weather pushed 7-m (23-ft) waves onto their boat and wrecked it. All six managed to get into a lifeboat, but they were still in great danger. Later, a small plane spotted the lifeboat almost 64 km (40 mi) from where the vessel had gone down. Rather than engage in a large search pattern taking many hours or days, the plane knew exactly where to fly and found the lifeboat just a few kilometers from where it was told it should be. The plane got its fix on the fishermen because of a satellite overhead.

This story has been repeated for hundreds of people in trouble all around the world. An aircraft crashes in a remote area. A race car driver runs off the road during a rugged cross-country race through wild country. Sailboats and yachts are battered by heavy seas during storms. In each event, time is critical. The survival rate is greater than 50 percent if rescuers arrive within twenty-four hours.

(Below left) Search and Rescue Satellites keep a watchful eye over the Earth for radio distress calls. (Below) Crewmen install an aerial high on the mast of the *Pride of Baltimore.* Every second, signals are sent to overhead satellites, enabling a close watch to be kept on the ship's course. Tragically the vessel was sunk in 1986 in a storm so fierce and quick that there was no opportunity to make use of the satellite connection.

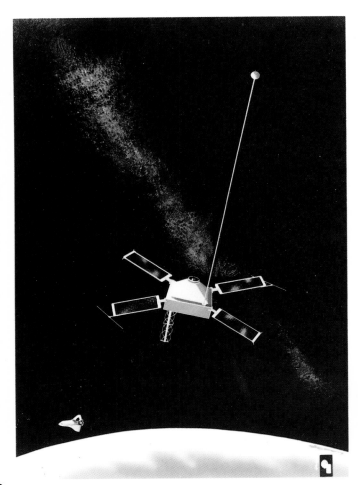

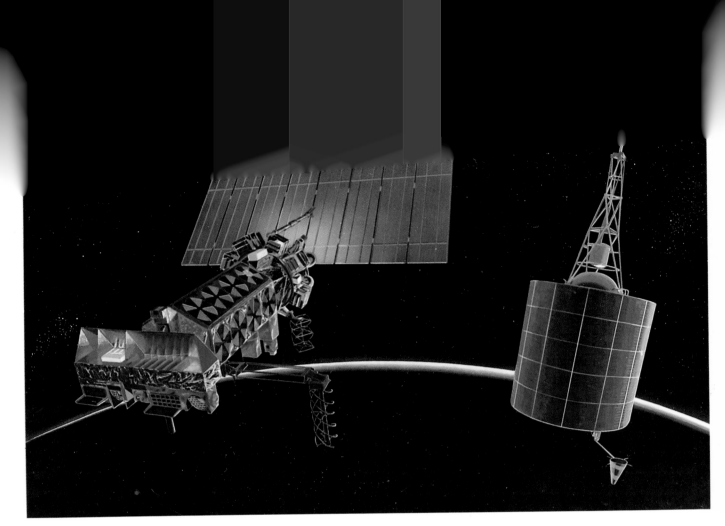

Help is available from outer space. Orbiting above the Earth are satellites that make up the COSPAS/SARSAT rescue satellite system. The satellites are operated by the Soviet Union and the United States. The name of the system is Search and Rescue Satellite-Aided Tracking. (COSPAS is the Russian-language acronym for the same thing.) How it works is relatively simple. When a ship gets into trouble, a radio beacon is activated on the vessel. The beacon has a very distinctive signal that sounds like no other radio message. The radio message is aimed upward and travels out into space. Eventually, one of the COSPAS/SARSAT satellites passes overhead and intercepts the signal. The satellite then relays that signal to the nearest ground terminal, triggering the rescue operation. Later, another satellite in the system may also receive the signal and relay it as well.

By knowing the exact position of the satellite at the time it received the signal and the direction the signal came from, a rescuer can get a "fix" on the beacon. The site of the accident can usually be pinpointed to within a 16- to a 24-kilometer (10- to 15-mile) radius. If two satellites receive the signal, an even more accurate fix can be made. An alert message is then sent to the search and rescue team nearest the accident location, and the rescue operation begins.

The major partners in the system are the Soviet Union, the United States, Canada and France, but Bulgaria, Finland, Sweden, Norway and the United Kingdom also participate. The result of this cooperation is that people's lives are being saved.

Two of the satellites in the COSPAS/SARSAT satellite rescue system are shown in this drawing. In real life, the two satellites are much further apart in order to increase their coverage of the Earth's surface.

THE HIGH GROUND

Satellites have provided many peaceful benefits for people on Earth. However, every new technology also has a dark side that could potentially be harmful. Spy satellites keep a close eye on military activities of other countries by monitoring atomic tests and observing the construction of missile launching sites. Ever since there has been war, the side that controlled the high ground had the advantage. Now, military planners are calling space the new "high ground."

ASAT means antisatellite. It is a device that seeks out satellites and destroys them. Many western space experts believe that the Soviet Union has an ASAT system ready to be used. The device consists of a maneuverable satellite that is placed in orbit by a booster rocket. Once in orbit, the ASAT chases its target satellite and gradually catches up to it many orbits and many hours later. When it gets near its target, the ASAT simply explodes and fragments blast into its target, ripping it to pieces.

The United States is the only other nation with ASATs, but the system is still experimental. However, it is much more sophisticated than the Soviet system. The American ASAT is actually a 5.2-m-(16 ft) long missile carried under the wing of an F-15 fighter plane. In tests, the F-15 has carried the missile thousands of meters above the Earth. When fired, the missile climbed to about 555 km (345 mi) and aimed itself on a collision course with an old satellite. With precise steering, the nonexplosive missile and its target satellite collided at a combined speed of more than 43,470 km/h (27,000 mph). The force of the collision was enough to destroy the satellite.

Incoming nuclear missiles are destroyed by X-ray laser beams in this computer drawing of a proposed "Star Wars" defensive satellite. A nuclear bomb in the satellite detonates, producing energy to power the laser.

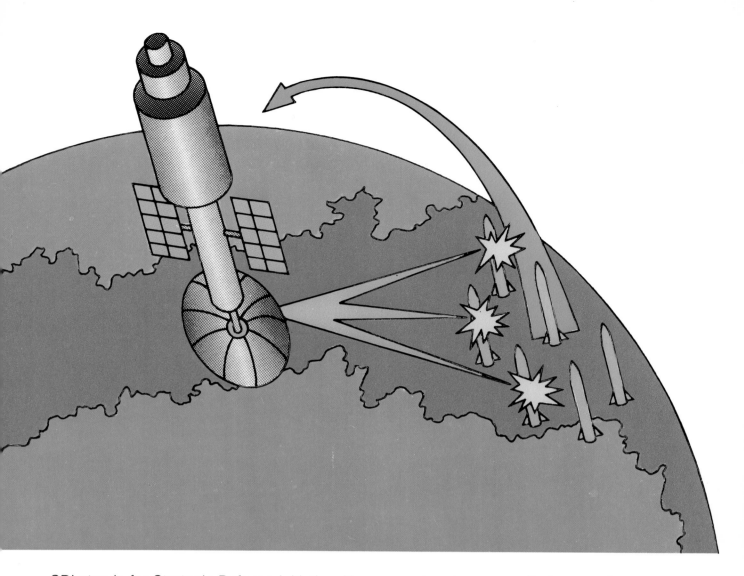

SDI stands for Strategic Defense Initiative. News reporters have called it the "Star Wars" plan. It is a very complicated plan to protect the United States from nuclear missile attack. Essentially, it is a string of satellites that will attack and destroy incoming missiles. In most versions of the plan, the satellites carry powerful laser weapons that will be directed at missiles during an attack. Shooting in straight lines across thousands of kilometers, the laser will cut through the missile walls and cause them to explode.

The purpose of SDI is to produce an umbrella that will keep missiles out like rain. The difficulties of achieving such a system are formidable. During an attack, hundreds of missiles would be launched at one time. Many would release clusters of warheads that would travel to separate targets. Laser satellites would have only minutes to shoot them down. In less than a second, they would have to locate a missile going at thousands of kilometers per hour, aim, fire a beam, and locate another target and do the same all over again. SDI is very controversial, and some experts believe it is too complicated to work.

ASATs and the SDI are frightening prospects for the use of outer space. They may reduce the possibility of war, but they may also encourage the building of new laserproof missiles. Both systems have become hotly debated topics at nuclear arms reduction talks between the United States and the Soviet Union.

During a nuclear attack this proposed defense satellite would use a mirror to aim powerful laser beams in order to destroy incoming missiles.

FIXING COSTLY MISTAKES

Launching satellites is a risky proposition. Satellites are expensive, sometimes costing hundreds of millions of dollars to build and launch. No matter how carefully the satellite is designed or how carefully the launch vehicle is checked out, something can still go wrong. The rocket's first stage may go off course and have to be destroyed. The second or third stage may malfunction, placing the satellite in the wrong orbit. The satellite itself may fail to function properly. Fortunately, most satellite launches occur without a hitch and the satellites operate for years in space without problems. But, when trouble hits, a financial disaster may result.

In the last few years, help for ailing satellites in orbit has arrived from a relatively new space launch vehicle, the Space Shuttle. The Shuttle is able to rendezvous with stray satellites in low orbits and send out a repair crew to fix them. If the satellite needs much more extensive repairs than can be accomplished in space, it will be brought into the Shuttle's payload bay for a return to Earth for an overhaul.

Astronauts Joe Allen and Dale Gardner prepare to bring a captured communications satellite back into the Shuttle's payload bay for a return to Earth.

Dale Gardner and Joe Allen work to store the PALAPA B-2 communications satellite in the Shuttle's payload bay for return to Earth. Like WESTAR VI, PALAPA B-2 also failed to reach its planned geostationary orbit.

Shuttle crews have successfully completed some important satellite rescue missions. In 1984 the ailing Solar Maximum satellite was repaired by space-walking astronauts George Nelson and James van Hoften after it had first been captured by the Shuttle's mechanical arm. The astronauts replaced a control module to prevent the satellite from rolling in space when it should point in one direction. They also removed small screws and reconnected many clusters of wires. Following the repair, the $75 million satellite resumed operation in space.

Dale Gardner pretends to hold a sale after he and Joe Allen stowed the WESTAR VI and PALAPA B-2 communications satellites in *Discovery*'s payload bay. Allen is seen reflected in Gardner's helmet visor.

THE NEXT GENERATION

Future satellites will be built in modules that can be assembled in different ways to meet different needs. They will be designed specifically to be serviced and refueled in orbit so that they can remain in space for many years. When repair is necessary, it will not always have to be carried out by space-suited astronauts. Instead, a robot repair satellite may be dispatched.

Many future satellites will be clustered together in large space platforms to save orbital space and cost. The platforms will have large solar cell panels and communication equipment to provide vital services for all their satellite tenants. This will make it much simpler to build the satellites because the necessary power and communications services will already be waiting in space.

One area of satellite use that will especially benefit from large platforms in space is the field of communications. Experts predict that demand for satellite communications will increase five times between the years 1980 and 2000. Unfortunately, most good locations for communications satellites are already taken up by older satellites. Just replacing them when they wear out won't be enough. Many more will have to be built and put into orbit. To eliminate congestion, very large satellites will be built.

A large, unfolding "maypole" communications satellite may make possible very small hand-held transmitters and receivers on Earth. ▶

Giant satellites with many square kilometers of flat surface may someday capture the Sun's energy and convert it into electricity for transmission to Earth by microwaves.

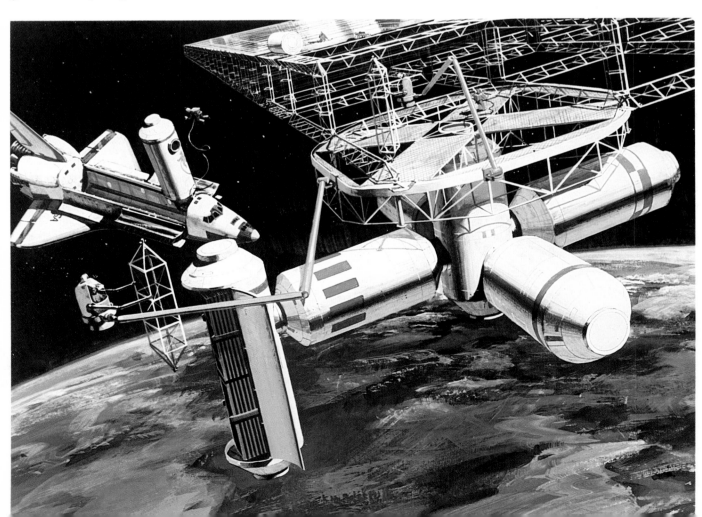

A future communications satellite might be as large as an entire city block. In some designs, hundreds of small antennas will be mounted on the platform, each aimed in a different direction. Large satellites are also looked upon as alternatives to new electric power plants on earth. Huge panels of solar cells will capture solar energy and convert it to electricity for beaming to Earth.

Satellites have been and will continue to be of great value to all people. Orbiting in the silent vacuum of outer space, satellites serve us on the ground by relaying our messages, by watching our atmosphere, by helping us to locate and protect our resources and by giving us clear glimpses of our universe.

(Left) The "dixie cup" communications satellite has many individually aimed antennas for future satellite postal service. (Below) The wristwatch of the future may actually be a wrist telephone connecting with any telephone in the world via giant communications satellites.

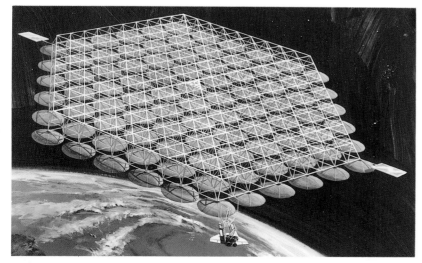

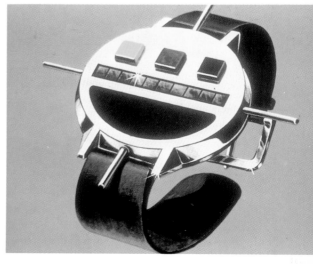

IMPORTANT DATES

October 4, 1957 The Soviet Union launches Sputnik 1, the world's first artificial satellite.

January 31, 1958 The Americans launch their first satellite, Explorer 1, into orbit.

November 3, 1957 Laika, the world's first living creature is launched into orbit.

December 18, 1958 The world's first communication satellite, Score, is successfully launched.

April 1, 1960 Tiros 1, the world's first weather satellite, is launched.

April 11, 1984 The Solar Max satellite is repaired in orbit.

November 11, 1984 The PALAPA communications satellite is retrieved from orbit and stowed on board the Space Shuttle for return to Earth and relaunch at a later date.

SATELLITE SCOREBOARD

	SATELLITES IN ORBIT	SATELLITES DECAYED
AUSTRALIA	3	1
BRAZIL	2	0
CANADA	14	0
CZECHOSLOVAKIA	0	1
EUROPEAN SPACE AGENCY	15	1
FRANCE	14	7
FRANCE/FEDERAL REPUBLIC OF GERMANY	2	0
FEDERAL REPUBLIC OF GERMANY	5	3
INDIA	7	2
INDONESIA	3	1
INTERNATIONAL TELECOMMUNICATIONS SATELLITE ORGANIZATION	35	0
ITALY	1	4
JAPAN	31	5
NORTH ATLANTIC TREATY ORGANIZATION	6	0
NETHERLANDS	0	1
PEOPLE'S REPUBLIC OF CHINA	4	14
SAUDI ARABIA	2	0
SPAIN	1	0
UNITED KINGDOM	9	6
UNITED STATES	520	563
UNION OF SOVIET SOCIALIST REPUBLICS	952	1267
TOTAL	**1629**	**1883**

Source: Office of Public Affairs, NASA Goddard Space Flight Center, August 1986.

GLOSSARY

ASAT Antisatellite weapon designed to destroy satellites in orbit.

Attitude Control System Equipment on a satellite that controls the direction in which it travels, keeping it properly aimed.

Communications System Equipment on a satellite, such as a receiver and antenna, that enables it to receive instructions from the ground and send back data.

COSPAS/SARSAT A Soviet and American satellite system that relays distress calls from ships and aircraft in trouble.

ESA European Space Agency. A group of thirteen nations joined together to conduct space research and technology applications. The nations include Austria, Belgium, Denmark, France, Germany, Ireland, Italy, the Netherlands, Norway, Spain, Sweden, Switzerland and the United Kingdom. Austria and Norway are associate members and will become full members on January 1, 1987.

EUTELSAT A European communications satellite system in orbit above Europe.

Geostationary, or Geosynchronous, Orbit A special orbit in which a satellite orbits at the same speed as the spinning Earth, thus remaining above the same point on the Earth at all times.

Hydrologist A scientist who studies the Earth's water supplies.

Infrared An invisible form of light that has a longer wavelength than red visible light.

IRAS Infrared Astronomical Satellite.

Landsat A NASA satellite that studies the Earth's landmasses and the features found on its surface.

Laser Light Amplification by Stimulated Emission of Radiation. A device for producing a pure, highly concentrated beam of parallel light.

Meteorologist A scientist who studies the Earth's atmosphere and weather.

Micrometeoroid A tiny grain of rock traveling through space at high speed.

MSS Multispectral scanner. An instrument on the Landsat satellite.

Orbit The path in which a satellite travels around the Earth, or the path in which a planet moves around the Sun.

Pixel Picture element. A single point on a picture that was taken by a satellite.

Polar Orbit A special satellite orbit that crosses the Earth's north and south poles.

Quasar Quasistellar object. Objects billions of light-years from Earth that emit tremendous amounts of light energy.

Satellite An object (natural or artificial) that orbits around a larger body in space.

Sputnik Russian word for satellite.

Ultraviolet Invisible light with wavelengths that are shorter than visible violet light.

X-rays High-energy form of invisible light with shorter wavelengths than ultraviolet light.

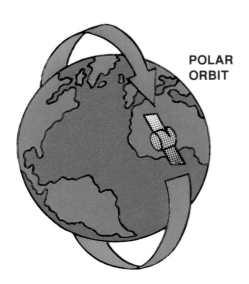

POLAR ORBIT

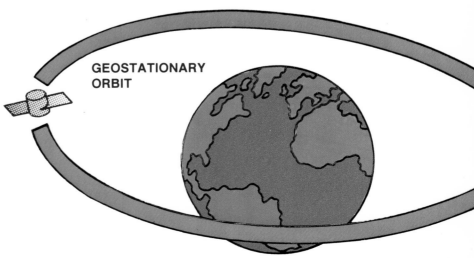

GEOSTATIONARY ORBIT

INDEX

Altitude control system, 9
Artificial satellite, early, 4–5
ASAT (antisatellite), 24–25
Astronomical satellites, 18–21

Biosatellite, 7

Canadian Communications Technology Satellite, 8
Communications satellites, 12–13, 27, 28–29
Computer system in satellites, 8
COSPAS/SARSAT rescue satellite system, 23
Crop production, satellite predictions, 17

Echo I and II, 12
Edwin P. Hubble Space Telescope, 18
Electrical energy for satellite, 9
Engineering Test Satellite, 8
European Space Agency (ESA), 10, 13
EUTELSAT system of satellites, 13
Explorer, 1, 6, 7

Geostationary Meteorological Satellite, 2, 11
Geosynchronous orbits, 12
Ground stations, 11

Helios-B, 9
Hydrologists, 16

Infrared satellites, 20
International Ultraviolet Explorer (IUE), 20
IRAS (Infrared Astronomical Satellite), 20–21

Jupiter C, 7

Landsat, 14–16
Long-distance phone calls via satellite, 13

Maypole communications satellite, 28
Meteorologists, 10
Meteosat, 10, 11
Micrometeoroids, danger of, 7–8

MSS (multispectral scanner), 15

Newton, Isaac, 4–5

PALAPA B-2, 27
Pictures of Earth, satellite, 14–16
Pixel, 16
Polar orbit, 10, 11
Pollution visible from space, 17
Power supply in satellite, 9

Redstone missile, 7
Repairing satellites in orbit, 26–27

Satellites
    first artificial, 5
    basic parts, 8
    camera systems, 10
    future, 28
    launchings, 26
    purpose of, 8
    range of, 8
SDI (Strategic Defense Initiative), 25
Seafood supplies, studying, 17
Search and rescue satellites, 22–23
Space race, beginning of, 5
Space shuttles, 13, 19, 26–27
Space Telescope, 18–19
Sputnik, 5, 6
Spy satellites, 24
Star Wars, 24–25

Telescopes on satellites, 18–19
Tracking and Data Relay Satellite (TDRS), 9

Vanguard rocket, 6, 7
Van Allen Radiation Belt, 7

Weather satellites, 10–11
WESTAR VI satellite, 26

X-rays from space, via satellites, 20

PRINTED IN BELGIUM BY
proost
INTERNATIONAL BOOK PRODUCTION